LET'S GET OUTDOORS!

Snowshoeing

by Kieran Downs

BLASTOFF! READERS 2

BELLWETHER MEDIA • MINNEAPOLIS, MN

Blastoff! Readers are carefully developed by literacy experts to build reading stamina and move students toward fluency by combining standards-based content with developmentally appropriate text.

Level 1 provides the most support through repetition of high-frequency words, light text, predictable sentence patterns, and strong visual support.

Level 2 offers early readers a bit more challenge through varied sentences, increased text load, and text-supportive special features.

Level 3 advances early-fluent readers toward fluency through increased text load, less reliance on photos, advancing concepts, longer sentences, and more complex special features.

★ **Blastoff! Universe**

Reading Level

Grade **K**

Grades **1–3**

Grade **4**

This edition first published in 2024 by Bellwether Media, Inc.

No part of this publication may be reproduced in whole or in part without written permission of the publisher. For information regarding permission, write to Bellwether Media, Inc., Attention: Permissions Department, 6012 Blue Circle Drive, Minnetonka, MN 55343.

Library of Congress Cataloging-in-Publication Data

Names: Downs, Kieran, author.
Title: Snowshoeing / by Kieran Downs.
Description: Minneapolis, MN : Bellwether Media, 2024. | Series: Blastoff! readers. Let's get outdoors! | Includes bibliographical references and index. | Audience: Ages 5-8 | Audience: Grades 2-3 | Summary: "Relevant images match informative text in this introduction to snowshoeing. Intended for students in kindergarten through third grade"– Provided by publisher.
Identifiers: LCCN 2023035135 (print) | LCCN 2023035136 (ebook) | ISBN 9798886878011 (library binding) | ISBN 9798886878950 (ebook)
Subjects: LCSH: Snowshoes and snowshoeing–Juvenile literature.
Classification: LCC GV853 .D68 2024 (print) | LCC GV853 (ebook) | DDC 796.9/2–dc23/eng/20230804
LC record available at https://lccn.loc.gov/2023035135
LC ebook record available at https://lccn.loc.gov/2023035136

Editor: Elizabeth Neuenfeldt   Series Design: Andrea Schneider   Book Designer: Josh Brink

Printed in the United States of America, North Mankato, MN.

Table of Contents

What Is Snowshoeing?

Snowshoeing is a winter activity.
People use snowshoes
to walk on snow.

Snowshoes fit over boots.
They keep people
from sinking into snow.

snowshoe

People snowshoe anywhere there is snow. Many snowshoers go to parks.

Favorite Snowshoeing Spot

Yellowstone National Park, Wyoming, USA

Claim to Fame

- miles of snowshoe trails
- guided hikes

Snowshoers walk through
many landscapes. Some people
snowshoe on mountains.
Others snowshoe through forests.

Walking on Snow

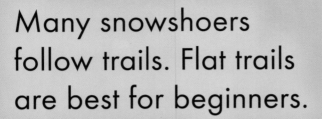

Many snowshoers follow trails. Flat trails are best for beginners.

Snowshoers can work their way up to longer and steeper trails.

Snowshoes are wider than shoes.
Snowshoers must take wide steps.

To climb hills, snowshoers step with their toes first. They use a **kick-step** in **powder** snow.

kick-step

Snowshoers step with their heels first to go down hills. They keep their weight back.

They **traverse** hills by keeping their weight uphill.

traversing a hill

Snowshoeing Gear

People wear different kinds of snowshoes. Longer snowshoes are used in powder snow.

Shorter snowshoes are used on packed snow. They are also used on steep or icy trails.

Snowshoe Sizes

longer snowshoes

shorter snowshoes

Snowshoers wear warm clothing. They carry food and water.

Snowshoe Gear

food and water

warm clothing

GPS device

poles

snowshoes

They use maps and **GPS** devices
to help find their way.
Poles help snowshoers **balance**.

Snowshoeing Safety

Snowshoers should always snowshoe with other people.

Snowshoers wear the right clothing. They should also have enough water.

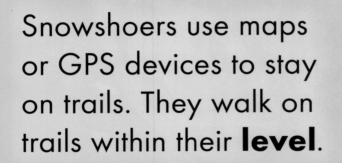

Snowshoers use maps or GPS devices to stay on trails. They walk on trails within their **level**.

↑ map

Snowshoers must be
aware of **hazards**.
They watch their step!

Glossary

balance—to stay steady and not fall

GPS—global positioning system; GPS is a system people use to find locations.

hazards—dangers or risks

kick-step—a kind of step in which snowshoers kick into the snow on a hillside to make a step to stand on

level—the amount of skill a person has

powder—related to light and dry snow

traverse—to travel across a hillside

To Learn More

AT THE LIBRARY

Leaf, Christina. *Cross-country Skiing*. Minneapolis, Minn.: Bellwether Media, 2024.

Owings, Lisa. *Hiking*. Minneapolis, Minn.: Bellwether Media, 2023.

Sabelko, Rebecca. *Mountains*. Minneapolis, Minn.: Bellwether Media, 2022.

ON THE WEB

FACTSURFER

Factsurfer.com gives you a safe, fun way to find more information.

1. Go to www.factsurfer.com.

2. Enter "snowshoeing" into the search box and click 🔍.

3. Select your book cover to see a list of related content.

Index